# WHISKEY

## A guide to the world's best distilleries and whiskeys

Parragon

Bath • New York • Cologne • Melbourne • Delhi
Hong Kong • Shenzhen • Singapore

This edition published by Parragon Books Ltd in 2018
and distributed by

Parragon Inc.
440 Park Avenue South, 13th Floor
New York, NY 10016
www.parragon.com



Written by Stuart Derrick
Designed by Plum5 Limited



Images courtesy of iStock

ISBN 978-1-4748-7131-0

Printed in China

# CONTENTS

# A SHORT HISTORY OF WHISKEY

*How a locally produced beverage for crofters in Scotland and Ireland has spread around the world to be enjoyed by billions.*

The first written record of whiskey production comes from Ireland in 1405. The Annals of Clonmacnoise record the death of a chieftain as being due to "taking a surfeit of *aqua vitae*" during Christmas.

*Aqua vitae*, or "water of life," was the term used in the Middle Ages for distilled spirits. The process of distillation began thousands of years ago, possibly with the Babylonians in Mesopotamia as far back as 2000 BCE. By the tenth century, Arab alchemists had discovered how to distill alcohol while making cosmetics. The word "alcohol" is derived from the Arabic *al-kuhl*, which describes a type of eye makeup.

Although, as Muslims, the Arabs did not drink alcohol, they brought the knowledge of distilling to Europe, where it gradually spread through religious orders, where distilled wine was used for medicinal purposes.

Because grapes were not readily available in Scotland, barley beer was distilled instead of wine. Barley grew easily in the damp climate of Scotland, but those same conditions made it difficult to store. Beer making was one way of using barley and making it last. The processes of beer and whiskey making are very similar up to the point of distillation, and by distilling beer into whiskey, a more potent brew was created that lasted even longer.

The name "whisky" (without an e in Scotland) derives from the Gaelic *usquebaugh*, which also means "water of life." Over time, it phonetically became "whisky." Whisky production in Scotland seems to have been in operation by the late fifteenth century.

Knowledge of distilling spread beyond the religious orders and became part of the farming year. It remained a cottage industry but was significant enough for the Scottish parliament to start taxing malt and whisky in the seventeenth century. Increasingly complex rates of taxation were applied following the Act of Union with England in 1707.

These taxes were widely seen as unfair and were accordingly flouted over the next 150 years as excisemen, known as "gaugers," and smugglers tried to outwit each other. Distillers produced whisky at night, when darkness hid the smoke from the stills, giving rise to the nickname "moonshine."

The excisemen fought a losing battle. By the 1820s, about 14,000 illicit stills were confiscated every year, yet more than half of the whisky consumed in Scotland was still untaxed. Finally, the 1823 Excise Act sanctioned the distilling of whisky in return for a

license fee of ten pounds, and a set payment per gallon distilled.

Now that the producers were on a legal footing, the quality of the product could be improved. This was aided by the invention of the column, or Coffey, still, which enabled the creation of lighter grain whiskies. This revolutionized Scottish whisky making in the 1840s and 1850s, when blenders, such as John Dewar, James Chivas, and George Ballantine, were able to take light-grain whiskies and blend them with heavier, peatier single malts from the pot stills.

Irish distillers produced their own version of whiskey, spelled with an "e" to distinguish it from Scotch.

Americans were also making their own whiskey by the late eighteenth century. Farmers found that it was a profitable way of converting surplus grain into a valuable product. European malt did not flourish in North America, so they turned to corn and rye, producing distinct American and Canadian whiskeys in the process.

Whiskey gained an advantage over other dark liquors, notably brandy, when the *Phylloxera vastatrix* vine louse devastated vineyards in France from the 1860s to the 1880s. Brandy and soda had been the drink of choice for the English middle classes. They now needed an alternative and whiskey met the criteria. Winston Churchill, who reputedly drank weak Johnnie Walker Black Label mixed with soda throughout the day, illustrated the generational change when he said: "My father could never have drunk whiskey except when shooting on a moor or in some very dull, chilly place. He lived in the age of brandy and soda."

Since then, whiskey has spread around the world. While Scotch maintains its claim on the liquor's heritage, whiskey is now a product of the world.

# HOW SCOTCH WHISKY IS MADE

*Whisky making produces an array of aromas, tastes, and colors, but they are all produced by a similar process using just three main ingredients: barley, water, and yeast.*

### *Malting*

Barley is soaked in warm water and allowed to begin germinating for about a week in a malting room (pictured right). This turns the starch contained in the barley to soluble sugars, which are later converted to alcohol. A number of different barley varieties are used for single malt whisky. The germination process is then halted by heating and drying, known as "kilning." Traditionally, ovens were fed with peat, giving malt whisky its distinctive, smoky flavor.

### *Mashing*

The dried malt is then ground in a mill and the resulting crushed "grist" is mixed with hot water in a mash tun. Sugars in the malt are dissolved in the liquid, which is now known as "wort."

### *Fermentation*

The resulting wort is transferred to washback vessels, where yeast is added to allow for fermentation and the creation of an alcoholic liquid called wash. Different kinds of yeast, such as brewer's yeast and distiller's yeast, are added in varying combinations by expert distillers to influence both yield and quality. The yeast converts the sugar in the wort to alcohol, resulting in a liquid that is about 8 percent ABV.

### *Distillation*

The wash is then distilled twice, in copper wash stills (pictured above). The stills are like large kettles where the wash is heated until it vaporizes and rises over the head of the wash still. The spirit is guided through condensers, which cool the vapor and return it to a liquid form in a second "spirit still," at which point it is known as "low wines." The process is then repeated in the spirit still in a slower form, with the liquid running into a locked spirit safe. Here, it is divided into three parts, based on alcohol quantity. The middle part is carefully extracted and stored in a spirit receiver, and this is the only part that becomes whisky.

### *Maturation*

This clear liquor is known as "new make" and has an ABV of 60–75 percent. Most malt whisky is cut (diluted) and filled into casks at 63.5 percent. It is now poured into

oak casks for maturation. Legally, it can't be called Scotch unless this period is at least three years (and is in Scotland). Many whiskies mature for much longer and acquire their distinct flavors and colors during this time. Scotch whisky may also have caramel coloring (E150A) added to give it a richer appearance.

### Grain whisky

The process for producing grain whisky is different. Grain whisky is an essential ingredient of blended whisky, which has the lion's share of the whisky market. It is, therefore, produced in huge quantities.

The mashing and fermentation process are the same as those used for malt whisky, although only about 10 percent of the mash recipe may be malted barley, with the bulk made up of wheat and corn. These grains are cooked prior to mashing to soften the grain starch and make it more soluble.

Grain whisky is then processed using a column still, which allows continuous distillation of spirit. This double column still has two components: an analyzer and a rectifier. The wash is pumped in at the top of the rectifier and flows down a coil, where it is warmed by the heat of vapors rising up the still. The wash then passes into the top of the analyzer, where it passes down through perforated plates. As it does, steam rises up, extracting alcohol vapors and taking them back to the bottom of the rectifier. These vapors then start to rise and are gradually condensed by the cool wash coils and the grain spirit extracted from the column.

It might sound complicated, but the result is an extremely efficient distillation process that creates grain spirit at about 94 percent ABV. It is then diluted to 68 percent ABV before being casked and matured, ready for the blending process.

# WHISKY OR WHISKEY?

*There are different types of whiskey worldwide. Which is which?*

### *Scotch whisky*

As the home of whisky, Scotland is very protective of its national beverage to the extent that the exact definition of "Scotch whisky" has been enshrined in UK legislation since 1909. Regulations provide added legal protection for the traditional regional names associated with Scotch production.

To qualify as Scotch whisky, the liquor has to have been distilled at a distillery in Scotland from water and malted barley, and matured in oak casks in Scotland for at least three years.

### *Irish whiskey*

Most Irish pot still whiskey is distilled three times, compared to twice for most Scotch. This results in a smoother taste—as well as the fact that peat is rarely used in malting. Irish whiskey must be distilled and aged in Ireland for a period of at least three years.

## *American whiskey*

Perhaps the best known American whiskey is bourbon from Kentucky. It must be made from a grain mixture dominated by corn and aged in new charred oak barrels. The fermentation process is often started by mixing in some mash from an older batch, a process known as "sour mash."

A variant, Tennessee whiskey, such as Jack Daniel's, is made in the state of Tennessee using a maple charcoal filter. American rye whiskey was the prevalent whiskey of the northeastern states, but largely disappeared after Prohibition. The rye gives what is described as a spicy or fruity flavor.

## *Canadian whisky*

This whisky must be distilled in Canada and aged for at least three years in oak casks. Like Scotch, it may contain caramel as a coloring agent. Canadian distillers first started using rye as a flavoring agent to provide a tang to their liquor; however, the primary grain used to make most Canadian whisky is corn, which is blended with rye grain whisky after distillation.

## *World whiskeys*

Whiskey or whisky is now produced in a bewildering array of countries, including Japan, India, Sweden, and Switzerland. Even Scotland's neighbor, England, is getting in on the act.

# THE AGE OF THE BLEND

*Following the introduction of Coffey's patent still in the mid-nineteenth century, distillers were able to produce huge amounts of an inexpensive, fairly bland liquor.*

Although some of this cheap, bland liquor was consumed by poorer people in Scotland, the majority of it was sent to England to make gin. Most malt whisky was still consumed in Scotland.

The mixing of whiskies from different distilleries had been in practice for some time, and whisky was mixed with herbs and other drinks to create a cheaper drink. In 1853, the Forbes-Mackenzie Act permitted the mixing of differently aged whiskies from the same distillery "under bond." This process, known as vatting, allowed distilleries to create more appealing and consistent blends of whisky.

One of the first distilleries to do so was Andrew Usher & Company, which that same year created Old Vatted Glenlivet, sometimes described as the first whisky brand. The 1860 Spirit Act opened the door farther to blends by permitting malts and grains to be blended under bond. These whiskies were cheaper to produce than malts, were more consistent, and had broader appeal.

Grain whisky was produced using a new and more efficient still, which created a much lighter style of liquor. This lighter liquor was combined with

the heavier malt whiskies to create blended whisky.

Andrew Usher, who created Old Vatted Glenlivet, is regarded as having perfected the art of the blend. At the time, mellower Irish whiskey was gaining in popularity in Great Britain, and some Scottish distillers started to create their own versions.

Usher's work in creating a more balanced, lighter, and drinkable whisky laid the foundations for Scotch whisky's growth. It also made him a fortune. By 1897, his North British Distillery was producing 3.5 million gallons of whisky a year and was the largest in Scotland.

This period saw the development of many of the great blended whisky brands, such as Johnnie Walker, Dewar's, Black & White, Chivas Regal, Ballantine's, and VAT 69. The repeal of the Navigation Acts in 1849 also created export opportunities in the colonies and dominions.

Blending whisky is a considerable art, because anywhere from fifteen to fifty malt whiskies, and two or three grains, are combined. The blender's task is to combine different single whiskies and produce a blend that brings out the best qualities of each of its constituent parts.

Every blend is different, not to mention secret; the proportion of malt whisky in each blend varies from 20–60 percent, and this will be reflected in the price.

The blender aims to produce a whiskey of recognizable character that will never vary from this consistent standard. This can be difficult, because the characteristics of the malts used will vary from year to year or may not be available at certain times, so the blender must make sure that the blend does not stray from the set formula.

Single whiskies are brought from the warehouse to the blending establishment, where an experienced blender mixes them. The blender is looking at how the various whiskies mix and the effect that has on the nose, the palate, and the finish. This is largely done through "nosing," or smelling, the whisky.

Having created the blend, the whisky is usually returned to the cask and left to marry for a period of months before being bottled. However, some companies prefer to vat their malts and grains separately, and they only bring the two together before bottling.

Although blended whisky makes up the bulk of the whisky market, it has never had the same cachet attached to malt whisky, and is often seen as the poor relation. However, in recent years this has changed slightly, because speciality whisky makers are creating more upmarket blends in an artisan fashion and with price tags to match.

Blended whisky has truly come of age.

# SCOTLAND

*Scotch whisky and Scotland are synonymous. The home of whisky's damp and cool climate may not always be welcoming, but it is ideal for producing two things that contribute to great whisky: barley and peat.*

It is no longer the only place that you can get great whisky, and some people contend that the Irish may have beaten the Scots to the punch in distilling it. However, history is written by the winners, and it's hard to dispute that whisky has delivered this small country in Northern Europe a winning hand.

Scotland exports 140 million cases to 200 countries worldwide and another 20 million casks lie maturing in warehouses in the country. There are 108 distilleries licensed to produce Scotch whisky, employing 10,000 people directly and 35,000 indirectly. Whatever way you look at it, Scotch whisky is a huge success.

It shouldn't be a surprise, therefore, that the description "Scotch whisky" is jealously guarded and refers only to whisky that has been made and matured in Scotland under strictly defined conditions. Although Scotch whisky has been produced for hundreds of years, the actual definition of what constitutes Scotch dates back to a 1905 court case in Islington in London. The case was brought by local authorities against two wine and spirit merchants for selling a "Fine Old Scotch Whisky" that was "not of the nature, substance and quality demanded" by the provisions of the 1875 Sale of Food and Drugs Act. At a time when grain whisky was in the ascendant, the drink was composed of 90 percent grain and 10 percent malt whisky.

The Islington authorities won the case, despite the merchants being supported by powerful distillers of grain liquor, but it led to a dissection of the question of what defined "whisky" by a royal commission. It reported in 1909 and determined that the term "Scotch whisky" covered malt, grain, and blended whisky.

Since then, Scotch whisky has been defined as a distilled liquor made

in Scotland from cereals, water, and yeast. It must have been stored in Scotland in oak casks no larger than 700 liters (185 gallons) for a minimum of three years.

Adhering to these conditions, hundreds of Scotch whisky brands have developed. Blended Scotch, such as Chivas Regal, Ballantine's, and Johnnie Walker, are among the biggest liquor brands in the world. Malts, such as Glenfiddich, Glenmorangie, and Highland Park, have helped drive the market even farther.

Malt whisky was once an ultra-niche product and was not truly exploited until the 1970s and 80s, when distillers started to wake up to its potential. Their marketing worked so well that blended whisky suffered by comparison, becoming regarded as something of a poor relation. In recent years, this process has been reversed somewhat, with blended brands fighting back due to new beverages that appeal to different customers.

Scotch whisky is divided into different regions: the Highlands, the Lowlands,

Speyside, Islay, and Campbeltown. Each of the regions is said to produce whiskies with their own unique characteristics. These days, it is sometimes debated whether such hard-and-fast definitions still hold true. Although the conditions in each region have historically helped define the whiskies produced there, some feel there is now more of a blurring of the lines.

Whatever the case, the future for Scotch whisky looks rosy, with continued demand leading to heavy investment in production. Global giants, such as Diageo, Pernod Ricard, and Bacardi, have poured billions into new and expanded facilities in Scotland, and they have the marketing and distribution clout to make Scotch successful around the world.

At a lower level, new players are also emerging, often reinvesting in old distilleries and warehoused whisky. Whatever the provenance of the producer, one thing is clear: The whisky is Scottish through and through.

# SPEYSIDE

Speyside, a region spanning Morayshire and the Highlands area, is the heartland of Scotch whisky production. Its rich alluvial soil and Gulf Stream-aided climate raise excellent barley, and many mountainous hideaways made it a hotbed of illicit distilling in the past. Now that the industry is legitimate, it is home to about two-thirds of the malt whisky distilleries in Scotland.

The first license to distill whisky legally in Scotland was granted in 1824 to George Smith and his son John Gordon Smith, of The Glenlivet distillery in Speyside. The Glenlivet style became so renowned that many distilleries adopted the name. Some were so far away that it led to a joke that The Glenlivet must be the longest glen in Scotland. The Smiths eventually registered the name in London in 1870, but despite legal proceedings, the descriptor "Glenlivet" was used by other distilleries for many years afterward.

Broadly speaking, Speyside whiskies fall into two groups. At one end of the spectrum there are the light, grassy whiskies, such as The Glenlivet; at the other end are rich, sweet, sherried whiskies, such as The Macallan and Glenrothes. Generally, the Speyside whiskies use only minimally peated barley and tend to be lighter than other Highland and Island whiskies, although there are exceptions, such as The BenRiach and Ballantruan.

However, there is no hard-and-fast rule to the characteristics of Speyside whisky, and the style has altered over time. Although more than half of Scotland's distilleries can be found in the region, the exact number is difficult to ascertain, because there is some dispute over whether some distilleries are Highland or Speyside. To add to the confusion, some distilleries that are usually thought of as Speyside declare themselves as Highland on their packaging; for example, The GlenDronach and anCnoc.

Certainly there are between fifty to sixty active distilleries in this region. What is indisputable is that the region's distilleries are responsible for producing some of the world's best-selling whiskies, such as Glenfiddich, Glen Grant, and The Macallan.

# LOWLANDS

Lowland whiskies were once predominantly used as a source for blending in Scotland, and by the late nineteenth century most production was for this purpose. The area has little or no peat, so its whisky is much lighter in style than that of other regions.

Because of their light, easy-drinking character, the whiskies from this area are sometimes known as the "Lowland Ladies." As well as being light in body and aroma, this feminine character shows itself in a fresh, grassy, and lemony nature, with flavor that may begin sweet but rapidly becomes dry.

Whereas in most whisky regions there is a blurring of lines in how a style tastes, Lowland whiskies are singular. As well as the lack of peat and salinity, this can be accounted for by the triple distillation of some Lowland whisky, notably Auchentoshan, creating a smooth drink.

Although there were once many distilleries in the Lowlands and Borders, their numbers declined as Highland and Speyside whiskies became more popular. Today, there are five malt-whisky distilleries operating in the Lowlands. Auchentoshan, Glenkinchie, and Bladnoch are the better known, and within their ranges hold at least one typical Lowland malt expression.

Three new Lowland distilleries have planned production in recent years. Ailsa Bay, sited at William Grant & Sons' Girvan distillery, released its first whisky in 2016. The whisky from Daftmill, a micro-distillery based on a working farm in Fife, is still maturing. Another project—to revive the Annandale distillery, which closed in 1919—is up and running, and put its first malt whisky in casks in 2014.

Lowland whisky from four closed distilleries can also still be found. Rosebank, which was mothballed by United Distillers in 1993, is generally considered to be the best Lowland malt. More rarely seen are St Magdalene from Linlithgow, Littlemill from Bowling, Dumbartonshire, and Ladyburn, from Girvan.

# HIGHLANDS

The Wash Act of 1784 determined differential excise levels for Highland and Lowland whiskies, as well as defining which was which. Anything distilled north of the "Highland line" between Greenock and Dundee is considered to be a Highland whisky.

As an exercise in definition, it's fairly blunt. As well as being the largest geographical area, the Highlands is also the hardest region to pin down in terms of style. Highland whiskies can vary greatly from light and delicate to full bodied and peated. As with all the other regions of Scotland, assigning a flavor profile to a whisky based on its geographical position is becoming outdated.

In the Northern Highlands, the distilleries north of Inverness are all coastal, except Glen Ord, which is only a couple of miles inland. This accounts for a slightly salty taste to Clynelish, Old Pulteney, and Balblair. Also in the north are the light and fragrant Glenmorangie, the sherried

Dalmore, and Glen Ord, which is sometimes held to be the best example of the Highland style.

The Southern Highlands produces lighter, fruitier, and drier whiskies, such as Edradour—from the smallest distillery in Scotland—and Aberfeldy. The Perthshire distilleries Glenturret, Tulliebardine, Aberfeldy, and Blair Athol lie in the fertile glens of the Tay and its tributaries. To the north is Dalwhinnie, and on the southern edge of the Highlands are Deanston, Glengoyne, and Loch Lomond distilleries.

In the Eastern Highlands, full-bodied, dry, fruity malts dominate. Apart from Glen Garioch, they have no smokiness. In the north of the region, Macduff and Knockdhu touch Speyside, producing whiskies that can be confused with that region. Farther south are Fettercairn and Glencadam, which produces a creamy, fruity malt. Royal Lochnagar and Glendronach sit between the Moray and the Tay.

The Western Highlands has a few distilleries still operational, including the coastal Oban and the Ben Nevis Distillery at Fort William.

# ISLAY

This small island off the west coast of Scotland is sometimes called "Whisky Island" due to its concentration of distilleries. There are eight working distilleries within its 240 square miles, and a ninth, Gartbeck, is planning to start distilling in 2018.

As the historic base of the regional kings known as the "Lords of the Isles," Islay has a history of independence, which is echoed in the unique flavors of its malt whisky. The island's topography has helped create some of the strongest-flavored malt whiskies. Islay has large areas of peat bog, so it is unsurprising that its malts are often high in phenols. Winter gales drive salt spray inland to saturate the peat, adding another distinction to Islay whisky. When used to dry the barley for Lagavulin, Ardbeg, and Laphroaig, the result is a powerful, almost medicinal taste, saturated with peat smoke, brine, and iodine.

To the north of the island, the distilleries produce a different whisky. Bruichladdich, which reopened in 2001, and Bunnahabhain draw spring

water before it has contact with peat. They also use lightly peated or unpeated barley, so their house-style whiskies are milder and lighter as a result. To confuse things, however, Bruichladdich also produces what it claims is the most heavily peated whisky in the world: Octomore.

The Bowmore distillery, in the middle of the island, has a taste somewhere between the northern and southern Islay whiskies. It has some peat but is not medicinal, with toffee and floral traces. Caol Ila is a briny, smoky whisky from Islay's biggest distillery. It is a relative newcomer as a single malt, and is a prominent malt used in many blends.

Finally, the island's newest distillery, Kilchoman, opened in 2005 and takes the Islay spirit of independence to the extreme, with all stages of production taking place on the island, including growing its own barley.

# THE ISLANDS

Strictly speaking, the Scottish islands are not a whisky region in their own right but are considered part of the Highlands region. However, the term is commonly used to describe the sparse scattering of whiskies produced in the islands around the Scottish mainland.

The Isle of Arran alone had about fifty legal and illegal distillers around 200 years ago. Over time, the number has declined dramatically, and now there are only seven distillers in all the Scottish islands; the whiskies are extremely diverse.

Arran's current distillery dates from 1995. Its delicate whiskies have recently come of age and are described as malty, rich, and fruity, with no peat.

On Jura, proximity to the sea leads to a slightly salty, smoky flavor in the oily and gently peated whisky of its one distillery. The Isle of Skye's distillery, Talisker, uses a peated malt, and the smoky, pungent whisky is similar in style to the peat monsters from Islay's southern coast.

Mull also has a solitary distillery, which produces Tobermory, a sweet, thick, slightly herbal whisky, and a heavily peated version called Ledaig.

To the north, Orkney's smoky single malts from Highland Park are coastal and full with plenty of honey, malt, and heather, while the other Orcadian distillery, Scapa, produces whisky that has a citrus and herbal quality.

# CAMPBELTOWN

Long before the musician Paul McCartney had heard of the Mull of Kintyre, the peninsula was famous for its whisky. Centered on Campbeltown, in the nineteenth century the area was producing around 925,000 gallons of liquor a year.

However, distillers could not keep up with the demand and quality plummeted, so much so that the whisky was sometimes referred to as "stinking fish." The fortunes of Campbeltown also took a downturn when its heavy whiskies lost favor and Prohibition in the United States hit sales.

Most distilleries have closed, and today only three of them remain in operation: Springbank, Glengyle, and Glen Scotia.

# IRELAND

*The Irish like to boast that they were the first to distill whiskey and that they shared the knowledge with their Scottish neighbors across the Irish Sea.*

If this is the case, they didn't make the most of their advantage, for it was Scotch whisky that went on to conquer the world while the Irish variant has had a tougher time until recently. Irish whiskey may be the smallest of the "big four" of Scotch, bourbon, Canadian, and Irish, but it is now the fastest growing of them all.

Irish whiskey must be made in Ireland and is typically a triple-distilled

liquor in contrast to the twice-distilled Scotch. Like Scotch, Irish whiskey is aged in wooden casks for a minimum of three years. The absence of peat in most of the better-known Irish whiskeys contributes to a smooth texture, and a fruity profile in the final spirit. Another important difference is that the Irish use unmalted as well as malted barley in the distillation process.

History has it that distilling was occurring in Ireland as early as the sixth century. At any rate, by the sixteenth century, whiskey was being produced by religious orders for consumption by the privileged.

Elizabeth I was reportedly fond of Irish whiskey, as was Peter the Great of Russia.

Home distilling was common prior to the Tudor settlement of Ireland, but in 1608 the state began to issue licenses for distilling. Among the first to be granted was a license for Antrim governor Sir Thomas Phillips to distill in the Bushmills region. The 1608 date is still printed on the labels of Bushmills whiskey, and Bushmills Distillery claims to be the oldest licensed distillery in the world.
By the late eighteenth century, about 2,000 stills were in operation, most of them illegal. When Victorian historian Alfred Barnard visited Ireland in 1885 to reseach for his book *The Whisky Distilleries of the United Kingdom*, only twenty-eight distillers were legal.

At the time, Irish whiskey was considered the best in the world and the "Big Four" Dublin distilleries of John Jameson & Son, John Power & Son, George Roe & Company, and William Jameson & Company had a combined output of 5 million gallons per year. In contrast, Scotland's distilleries were trivial affairs, with an average production of 119,000 gallons.

This would prove to be a high watermark for Irish whiskey. The patent still may have been perfected by an Irishman, Aeneas Coffey, but Irish distillers stuck to their pot stills, while the Scots eagerly adapted this more efficient means of distilling. Meanwhile, the institution of the Irish Free State in 1922 led to trade embargoes that shut off the Irish distillers' main market in Great Britain and its empire. At the same time, the arrival of Prohibition in 1920 in the United States marked the end for many Irish whiskey makers.

Distillers Jameson, Power, and Cork survived by consolidation, forming the Irish Distillers Group in 1966. They gradually closed their old sites and moved production to a new state-of-the-art plant in Midleton. At this low point, production had probably dropped to fewer than 500,000 cases a year.

However, from here the comeback started. In 1987, the first new Irish distillery for more than a century appeared when the independent Cooley Distillery was founded near Dundalk. The company was bought by Jim Beam in 2011.

At the same time, other liquor players, such as Diageo, William Grant, and Illva Saronno, started investing—suddenly Irish whiskey was sexy. The result has been two decades of steady growth, with sales building to 6.5 million cases in 2013.

It's not just the big players that are benefiting. Dingle Distillery opened in May 2013 as a craft producer of artisan whiskey. Niche Drinks is building a £15 million ($24 million) distillery in Londonderry, while Walsh Whiskey Distillery is investing €25 million ($27 million) in expansion.

# BUSHMILLS

Bushmills distillery, near the Giant's Causeway in Northern Ireland, was founded in 1784, making it one of the oldest distilleries in the world. It is the second best-selling Irish whiskey, but it had to overcome challenges, including a fire that destroyed the site in 1885 and the decline of the Irish whiskey sector from the 1900s. Dozens of Irish whiskey distillers disappeared, but Bushmills has clung on until the sector began its comeback in the 1980s.

The distillery benefited from huge investment from its owner Diageo, which, combined with excellent advertising that emphasized its distinct smoothness, and a fashion for all things Irish, powered Bushmills in markets around the world. Bushmills produces only malt whiskey, which it triple distills in traditional copper pot stills.

Its malt whiskeys include ten-, sixteen-, and twenty-one-year-old single malts, as well as two core blends: Bushmills Original and Black Bush. Numerous limited releases have also been produced over the years.

# JAMESON

John Jameson started making whiskey in 1780 at the Bow Street distillery in Dublin. His commitment to quality quickly established the company as a leading player, and by 1820, Jameson had become Ireland's second biggest distilling company. Jameson's fortunes rose and fell with those of the Irish whiskey industry over the next century, but in 1966 it was part of a bold move to secure its future.

Irish Distillers was formed by the four distilling companies that had survived. Combining their resources was considered a better way of growing the industry. In 1975, a new distillery was built on the site of the old Midleton distillery in County Cork. Although it brought to an end nearly 200 years of distilling in Dublin, it helped Jameson become the top Irish whiskey and one of the top twenty best-selling whiskies in the world.

As well as being a feat of engineering genius, capable of producing the multiple liquor styles to replicate the brands of the distilleries it replaced, Midleton distillery produces its own whiskey. Midleton is a premium whiskey released only once a year in limited quantities, hence its name, Midleton Very Rare.

# NORTH AMERICA

*More than eighty years after the end of Prohibition in 1933, Americans have a renewed thirst for bourbon, rye, corn whiskey, and Tennessee whiskey. Such is the clamor that some in the industry have reported future supply worries, because the market sector struggles to keep up with rampant demand.*

There are several reasons contributing to the good news for American whiskeys. Some point to the retro appeal of TV shows such as *Mad Men*, where the characters happily knock back hard liquor. Others say that the "straight" nature of bourbon and other whiskeys, in that they are pure drinks with a sense of heritage and no additives, plays well in marketing terms.

American whiskey started its life as a raw, unaged liquor, distilled to fortify the early colonists of the new frontier. It took many years before it developed into the distinctively American bourbons, ryes, and Tennessee whiskeys of today.

The earliest liquor drunk by settlers had to be imported from Europe. This was obviously costly and Americans were soon trying to produce their own liquor. An early innovation was the use of rye instead of barley, which did not crop well. Over time, the native corn was also introduced.

Until the mid-eighteenth century, whiskey was made in relatively small quantities, mainly by farmer-distillers. It was an ideal way of using surplus grain, and the end result was certainly easier to transport.

Whiskey achieved a higher profile when President George Washington took a particular interest in the liquor. As well as suggesting that public distilleries be constructed to service the needs of the army, he distilled his own rye whiskey.

In Kentucky, distillers were busily creating what some see as the United States' only native beverage: bourbon. The first commercial distillery was opened in 1783 by Evan Williams, while Elijah Craig's decision to char corn whiskey is seen by some as a defining moment in the creation of bourbon.

Neighboring Tennessee went off on its own direction after the invention

of the Lincoln County Process. This filtration system sees the whiskey pass through maple charcoal and is held to account for the mellower flavor of whiskeys, such as Jack Daniel's.

There was room for both liqours over the next century, as the whiskey industry grew and became more sophisticated. Prohibition, from 1920 to 1933, almost put an end to them. However, as well as huge illicit production and smuggling of whiskey, some distilleries carried on producing whiskey for "medicinal" purposes.

When Prohibition ended, the U.S. whiskey industry started to recover. It had stiff competition, because Canadian and Scotch whisky had gained a valuable foothold, as had clear liqours, such as gin. However, it has gradually made a comeback, with clever marketing and a focus on quality. The world soon began to recognize American brands.

The craft of American whiskey making led one whiskey guru, Jim Murray, the author of the best-selling *Jim Murray's Whiskey Bible*, to proclaim that bourbon had overtaken Scotch, and that the best whiskey was now coming from Kentucky, where Buffalo Trace was "arguably the best distillery in the world."

# KENTUCKY

Kentucky is famously the home of bourbon whiskey, producing 95 per cent of the world's supply. The liquor doesn't have to be made there—many U.S. craft distilleries produce their own versions—but the big names, such as Jim Beam, Maker's Mark, Wild Turkey, and Four Roses, all hail from the bluegrass state.

As the saying goes, all bourbon is whiskey, but not all whiskey is bourbon. To qualify as straight bourbon, the liquor has to be distilled in the United States from at least 51 percent corn, and aged in charred new oak barrels for at least two years. Only water may be added before bottling.

Bourbon production started in Virginia, before Kentucky became a separate state, in the 1700s. Corn cultivation in the area had been encouraged by Virginia's "corn patch and cabin rights," which gave free land to settlers who grew the crop. It was easy to cultivate and it also made a distinctive style of whiskey, lighter than the rye whiskey from the East.

Many of the brands associated with bourbon production today date from the late 1700s. Jacob Beam (Jim Beam) built his first distillery in 1788. Robert Samuels (Maker's Mark) arrived in 1780. Elijah Pepper (James E. Pepper and Old Crow) settled in Old Pepper Springs, Kentucky, in 1776.

The name "bourbon" refers to Bourbon County, which was stamped as a place of origin on barrels of the liquor. Bourbon's place in U.S. history was officially recognized by Congress in 1964, when it was declared a distinctive product of the United States.

In recent years, demand has soared and production has risen more than 120 percent since 1999 to more than a million barrels in 2012. However, a side effect of this success is that most of the big producers have been bought up by foreign owners.

Although bourbon reigns supreme in Kentucky, the state also produces some rye whiskeys, such as Sazerac Rye, produced by Buffalo Trace, and Knob Creek Straight Rye. Just don't try making a mint julep with them.

JACK DANIEL'S
Tennessee
HONEY

# TENNESSEE

Historically, making whiskey was a well-practiced pursuit in Tennessee. By 1799, there were sixty-one stills recorded in Davidson County alone, serving a population of just 4,000. Today, there are only about four producers, although one—Jack Daniel's—is among the biggest liquor brands in the world.

While most drinkers would describe Jack Daniel's as bourbon, that's not what it's called on the bottle. Jack Daniel's, Collier and McKeel, and George Dickel are the three best-known brands of Tennessee whiskey (or whisky, as George Dickel spells it). It is a type of bourbon, but it is legally required to be "a straight Bourbon Whiskey authorized to be produced only in the State of Tennessee," according to the North American Free Trade Agreement (NAFTA).

As of May 2013, it is also required that Tennessee whiskeys are made using the Lincoln County Process of filtration through a layer of maple charcoal before it is barreled.

Proponents of the process claim it mellows the whiskey, allowing vanilla, caramel, and licorice flavors to emerge. Ironically, following the alteration of county boundaries, the only Tennessee whiskey that is still actually made in Lincoln County, Benjamin Prichard's, does not follow the process, because it has a legal exemption.

Until 2009, only three of the ninety-five counties in Tennessee permitted distilling. However, after legal changes, forty-four counties allow distilling, and small artisan brands of whiskey are starting to emerge, such as Nashville's Corsair Artisan, Peg Leg Porker bourbon, and Cumberland Cask.

These are producing on a small scale for whiskey connoisseurs and will have to go some way before they threaten the Moore County giant. Jack Daniel's sold 11 million cases of the classic Black Label in 2012–13 and is investing $100 million to boost production further. However, drinkers will still have to leave its Lynchburg home to sample the actual liquor, because this is a dry county.

# CANADA

Settlers in what was then known as New France started distilling their own liquor as early as 1668, under colonial administrator Jean Talon. The first Canadian distillery was opened in Quebec City in 1769, and by the 1840s, there were more than 200.

Canadian whisky (without an e) is generally a multigrain blended style of whisky that is smoother, sweeter, and lighter than other whisky styles. To qualify as Canadian whisky, it must be produced and aged in Canada for at least three years in wooden barrels, and be at least 40 percent ABV.

The whisky is colloquially known as rye; however, it is seldom made from 100 percent rye. The early settlers grew rye grain because it thrived in poor soil and was used for making whisky. They shifted to distilling with wheat when it became the principal grain of the prairies, although they retained some rye as a flavoring agent. This practice remained when distillers switched to corn as their main grain.

Canadian whisky saw strong growth in the nineteenth century, with entrepreneurs, such as Hiram Walker, founder of Canadian Club, and Gooderham and Worts producing whisky on an industrial scale. Their products found a ready market in the United States, where Canadian whisky had such a high reputation that some local producers tried to pass off their whiskey as Canadian.

Some hold that Canadian distillers benefited from Prohibition in the United States, but Canada also had a brief period of prohibition, although it did not overlap with that of the United States. Ironically, today smuggling from the United States into Canada is a problem due to the disparity in alcohol duties.

Although Canadian whisky's flavor profile makes it ideal for mixing, its reputation has suffered in recent years because some have labeled it as lacking in taste. However, the industry is fighting back with new straight rye, spiced, and small-batch whiskies. Connoisseur blends, such as Lot 40, Forty Creek, and Century Reserve, are helping Canadian whisky regain some of its reputation.

# JAPAN

*Despite being a relative newcomer to whisky making, Japan is now the second-biggest producer of single malt whisky in the world.*

Japan's ranking among whisky nations rose when Suntory bought Jim Beam for $16 billion in 2014. The deal made Suntory the third-largest liquor company in the world. As well as acquiring the world's biggest-selling bourbon, it also now owns Teacher's, Laphroaig, and Canadian Club.

It's the latest chapter in the story of a long love affair with whisky. It started in 1854, when Commodore Matthew Perry, the U.S. commander who negotiated the treaty to open up Japanese trade to the West, brought about 130 gallons of whiskey as a gift for the emperor.

Inventive Japanese bevereage makers tried to replicate the taste of foreign liquor, initially without great success. A liquor known as *yoshu* was distilled as early as 1870, but commercial production of whisky did not commence until 1924. This was when Shinjiro Torii established Kotobukiya Limited—later renamed Suntory—the first distillery in Japan.

Torii employed another Japanese whisky pioneer, Masataka Taketsuru, to help him. Taketsuru had traveled to Scotland in 1918 to study the secrets of making whisky, and would eventually strike out on his own in 1934, when he founded a distillery at Yoichi on Hokkaido. This would later become Nikka (factory pictured below), which produces Yoichi 20-year-old.

The Scottish influence on Japanese whisky making continues to this day, and the Japanese spell whisky the Scottish way. Distilleries use malted barley instead of corn or rye, and whiskies are crafted in a Scottish style that echoes Lowland and Speyside varieties, generally avoiding the heavy smoke, peat, and saline flavors. Japanese oak is unique to Japanese whisky production and is used in a handful of whiskies to create rich fruit flavors.

Although initially Japanese whisky was produced for the home market, in recent years it has been increasingly lauded as world class. Today, Japanese whiskies are popular as a style of their own and exports have increased, while Japan's distilleries' attention to detail has helped them win a barrelful of top international awards. It is not uncommon for Japanese single malts to outperform their Scottish counterparts in blind tastings.

Part of the reason may be that Japanese distillers have had to be more experimental in order to produce better blended whisky. In Scotland, blends are created by bringing together different malts from an array of distilleries to produce the perfect whisky. In Japan, companies are reluctant to trade with their competitors, so a blended whisky will generally only contain malt whisky from their own distilleries, sometimes supplemented with imported Scottish malts. Because of this, individual distilleries in Japan are adept at producing a more diverse range of whiskies.

When it comes to drinking whisky, the Japanese are eager on pairing it with food. Usually, this is done in the form of a watered whisky or a highball, an easy-to-drink concoction of one part whisky and two to three parts soda. It has become so commonplace that it is sold in cans in convenience stores and on draft in bars as an alternative to beer. Different whiskies can be mixed with different courses, including sushi, sashimi, tempura, and even sweet courses.

Single malt is typically served on ice, but not just any ice. Connoisseurs will seek out a bar where the bartender is adept at serving whisky with an ice ball. This is a large ball of ice that chills the whisky without overdiluting it. The bartender carves the ice ball, and puts it into a glass of water to cool the glass. The water is then discarded and the bartender pours whisky on top of the ball and rolls it to homogenize the temperature. The Japanese are nothing if not obsessive about detail.

# THE REST OF THE WORLD

*For many years, whiskey has been enjoyed around the world, but it was only produced in Scotland, Ireland, the United States, and Canada, with Japan a recent addition. However, that's not the case today.*

In recent years, the picture has started to change dramatically, as countries that have always enjoyed a dram started to produce their own. Some are linked to Great Britain, such as India, South Africa, and

Australia, but many new whiskey producers have no such history.

From France and Finland to Taiwan and Tasmania, whiskey distilleries are cropping up around the world. Just as the craft-beer movement has spread around the world, whiskey making is now being attempted by global whiskey aficionados. The results are fascinating, because although the basic process of distilling is the same around the world, new producers are doing things their own way, and in the process they are coming up with new tastes and expressions.

In the not-so-distant past, a list of the top 100 whiskies would have been dominated by Scotch whisky, with a few other names from the major whiskey producers. Although Scotch still sets a benchmark, the rest of the world is catching up quickly and new whiskeys are increasingly hailed as the equal of, if not superior to, Old World whiskey.

Budding whiskey manufacturers have realized that there is no point in trying to produce a facsimile of Scotch single malt. Instead, companies such as Mackmyra have

tried to do something different—for example, using juniper branches and peat to malt barley, aping the use of juniper in Swedish cuisine. They have also experimented with the use of fresh Swedish oak barrels.

Welsh whiskey producer Penderyn uses a single-still system designed by David Faraday, a descendant of the Victorian scientist Michael Faraday. While most Scottish and Irish distilleries use a conventional two- or three-pot still system, the technology developed at Penderyn allows for an extremely clean, flavorful liquor to be produced from a single still. The barley wash is supplied by Welsh brewer Brains, and the spirit is aged in Buffalo Trace bourbon casks before finishing in Madeira, sherry, port, or old Islay whisky barrels.

Different climates are also helping new whiskey producers to come up with different flavors. The hot temperatures in India and Australia help whiskey mature at a much faster rate. As well as leading to interesting new flavor profiles, it also provides the opportunity for whiskey producers in these countries to get their product to market more quickly. Whiskey is a long-term investment, and the earlier producers can start to make a return on their money, the better.

Financial constraints haven't stopped new enthusiasts coming on board. One of the latest is Puni Distillery in the north of Italy. The family-owned company started making liquor in 2012 and had its first malt whiskey bottled by 2015. In true Italian fashion, the distillery is something of a design statement, housed in a 43-foot-tall, red brick cube designed by architect Werner Tscholl.

Other projects have been seen in Argentina, where a micro-distillery emerged in Patagonia. La Alazana started in 2011 and had whiskey ready by 2014. Israel's Milk and Honey Distillery raised more than $1million to produce single-malt whiskey by the Dead Sea. Meanwhile, New Zealand bottler Thomson Whisky has taken the step to distill its own liquor.

Making whiskey is not for those with a short-term mentality. Some of the best whiskeys in the world were laid down forty or fifty years ago by people who may never have sampled them when they were bottled. New whiskey makers around the world are at the start of a long journey, during which they will make many discoveries and some mistakes. The more they learn about their craft, the better the results. With whiskey, time is a vital ingredient.

# EUROPE

Europe has always been an important market for Scotch whisky, particularly in recent years, because the beverage has been in long-term decline in its home market.

Now Europeans are starting to produce their own versions of one of their favorite beverages. New distillers are springing up all over Europe, from England and Wales to France and down to Spain. There is even a whiskey distillery in Switzerland.

Most are small and some have distilled previously or continue to distill other spirits. Others have jumped in at the deep end without having any previous experience. The whiskeys are generally produced for the local market but some are expanding their ranges and are looking to export.

Although most of the European players are fairly new, some have a longer history, such as Spain's Destilerias y Crianza del Whisky (DYC). The company started producing whiskey in 1959 and is now the best-selling brand in its home market, with production of 610,000 gallons a year. It also

offers single malts. Most European distilleries are not on the same scale, but their ambitions of producing a quality whiskey are equally serious. England's St George's distillery opened in 2006 with its first release, or chapter, as it calls each whiskey, in 2010. To date it has produced thirteen small-batch chapters, picking up numerous awards along the way.

Sweden's Mackmyra is one of the best examples of European whiskey made good. It commenced production of malt whiskey in 1999 and now has several expressions available. In 2012 it was named European Spirits Producer in the International Wine and Spirit Competition in London. The company has floated on the Swedish stock exchange and moved to a new distillery with a capacity of 265,000 gallons.

And new micro-distilleries continue to emerge. In 2013, the first whiskey distillery in London for more than a century began production. The first dram from the London Distillery Company is predicted to be a fruity, light number with malt, chocolaty, and caramel notes.

# SOUTH AFRICA

As a wine-producing country, it's not surprising that brandy is the favored liquor in South Africa; however, whiskey comes a strong second.

According to a report by consultancy DNA Economics, "Compared to other international markets, South Africa displays disproportionately high consumption of premium and super-premium whiskey." In other words, South Africans prefer the good stuff.

Whiskey consumption was up by 9 percent between 2010 and 2011, according to researcher South African Wine Industry Information & Systems. The drink now accounts for 6 percent of all alcohol consumed—the highest since the mid-1990s.

Traditionally, this has been good news for Scotch whisky, with brands such as Bell's and J&B being the tipples of choice. However, imports are suffering at the hands of local production, with Distell, South Africa's largest local whiskey producer, claiming that its strongest growth in spirits comes from whiskey and cognac.

The company blends Scottish malts and South African whiskey for its Harrier and Knights brands, and it has seen great success with two of its other homegrown brands. Three Ships, from the James Sedgwick distillery, has won international accolades, including the title of World's Best Blended Whisky at the 2012 World Whiskies Awards in London.

Plaudits have also been heaped on Bain's Cape Mountain Whisky, which won Gold in the 2012 and 2013 International Wine & Spirit Competition in London. It was launched in 2009 and is also produced by James Sedgwick, which makes malt and grain whiskey on the same site.

Encouraged by the response to local whiskey, other new entrants are emerging. Drayman's is a Pretoria-base craft brewer that has turned its attention to liquor. A *solera* whiskey is already available, and a single malt is currently maturing.

# INDIA AND THE FAR EAST

Scotch whisky manufacturers cast an envious eye over the Indian market. It is one of the fastest-growing markets for spirits in the world, but one they have limited success in reaching because of high import duties.

With imported whiskeys out of reach for many in the population, people have turned to locally produced "whiskeys." Spirits have been distilled in India since the time of the Raj, but in reality many today are closer to being rums, consisting of a relatively small amount of malt whiskey. In fact, much of the whiskey produced is molasses-based.

As well as being a potential gold mine, the Indian market is also a headache for the Scotch whisky industry, because of the manner in which producers play fast and loose with their descriptions of "whisky" and "Scotch." The Scotch Whisky Association, the guardian of Scotch's global reputation, had 100 trademark oppositions and several legal cases underway in India in 2012, according to its legal report for that year.

The bulk of Indian whiskey is for local production, but there are signs that a few producers are looking farther afield with more finessed offerings. Bangalore-based Amrut Fusion has gained a wider appreciation after scoring highly with whiskey critics.

Meanwhile, John Distilleries, the sixth-largest distiller in the world, released Paul John in 2012 to a pleasantly surprised world. The Goa-based company has now produced seven expressions, including its first two, Edited and Brilliance.

Beyond India, Taiwan has become an emerging force in whiskey manufacture. Kavalan is produced by the spirits arm of the King Car industrial group, which has interests in beverages, food, biotechnology, and aquaculture, among others. The first bottle of Kavalan was released in December 2008 and exports started in 2012.

The Taiwanese are big whiskey lovers and the Kavalan distillery is a multimillion investment with a visitor center that welcomes one million enthusiasts a year. The fledgling operation is also on the doorstep of China, one of the world's emerging whiskey markets.

# AUSTRALIA AND NEW ZEALAND

Although there is no record of the first distilleries in Australia, the colony has probably been producing hard liquor since soon after the arrival of European settlers in 1788. At any rate, by 1796, governor John Hunter was complaining of the widespread number of "illicit distilleries of spirituous liquors."

As the distilling industry became established during the nineteenth century, distillers favored rum and gin over whiskey, which tended to be imported. There were attempts at creating an Australian dram, notably Corio, but it is not fondly remembered, earning the description of "gut rot." It ceased production in 1989.

Around that time a new generation of Australian whiskey makers came to the fore. Led by Tasmania's Bill Lark, they focused on quality over quantity. Lark decided that conditions on the island were perfect for whiskey making, and set about overturning Tasmania's century-and-a-half-long ban on distilling. Today, Lark Single Malt is one of around ten whiskeys produced on Tasmania.

Overall, there are more than twenty active whiskey distilleries in Australia producing a range of styles. Many are bottled at cask strength and are typically nonchill filtered. Sullivan's Cove has received accolades as one of the best world whiskeys, and the Nant Distillery was rated as the maker of one of the top fifty whiskeys in the world.

Neighboring New Zealand has also caught the whiskey bug, which is perhaps not surprising, given its purported similarities in climate and terrain to Scotland. Early distilling seems to have been initiated by Scottish settlers in 1838, and thrived particularly in the Dunedin and Otago region until the government cracked down in the 1870s.

After many years of imports, today's whiskeys are relatively small-scale from distillers such as Kaiapoi, which produces a thirteen-year-old malt, and Hokonoi, whose single malt, the Coaster, uses driftwood and seaweed to malt barley.